nirvana in a nutshell

nirvana in a nutshell

157 ZEN
MEDITATIONS

Scott Shaw

Red Wheel

Boston, MA / York Beach, ME

First published in 2002 by
Red Wheel/Weiser, LLC
York Beach, ME
With offices at:
368 Congress St.
Boston, MA 02210
www.redwheelweiser.com

Cataloging-in-Publication Data available upon request from the Library of
Congress.

Typeset in Bembo.

ISBN 1-59003-017-6

Printed in Canada
TCP

09 08 07 06 05 04 03 02
 8 7 6 5 4 3 2 1

Introduction

NIRVANA, the state of grace where the individual merges with the cosmic whole and there is no longer any physical suffering, mental anguish, or unanswered questions.

NIRVANA, the state of holy union where the limitations of the physical self fall away revealing the Buddha nature hidden within all of us.

NIRVANA, the word conjures up images of a garden of eden paradise with pristine blue skies, crystal clear streams, beautiful flowers covering the landscape, and saintly robed beings walking peacefully through the gardens.

NIRVANA, the understanding which so many people, through out history, have sought after. Some have renounced the world, gone into seclusion, passed their days lost deep in meditation in the caves of the Himalaya. Others have walked for untold miles, bowing with each step, seeking to gain a glimpse of the infinite.

NIRVANA, why does it seem so distant when we are told it is something we already possess?

NIRVANA is distant because it has been proclaimed as distant.

NIRVANA is not known, because it has been propagated as the ultimate obtainment — fathomable only by the most holy.

NIRVANA is remote because the untruth has been passed on for generations, by the unenlightened, that years of formally structured ascetic training must take place before you can even hope to grasp even the slightest glimpse of pure cosmic consciousness.

NIRVANA has been made a desire. And, as Siddhartha Guatama, the Sakyamuni Buddha, profoundly stated, "The cause of suffering is desire."

Desires remove you from the absolute. Desires remove you from knowing. Desires keep you from NIRVANA — because desires make you believe that you do not possess something, thus you are trapped by seeking its obtainment.

Take a few moments to read through these pages, let go of your desires, begin to embrace inner peace, and NIRVANA will not be so distant, so desired, so far off. It will become who you are.

> *NIRVANA is.*
> *You are.*
> *Let yourself experience this truth.*

one

What has kept you from Nirvana?

> Is it because you are not a monk?
> Is it because you are not in India, Thailand, Japan, or Tibet?
> Is it because you do not meditate enough?
> Is it because you are a bad person?
> Is it because you developed negative Karma in a past life?

> *Nirvana is.*
> *You are.*
> *Be enlightenment.*

two

Is Nirvana something you get,
  or is Nirvana something you are?

If you can get it, you can lose it.
  If you are it, it is never gone.

three

People do all kinds of things to find Nirvana:
> they meditate,
> they pray,
> they give up material possessions,
> they refrain from sex,
> they live in caves.
> They do strange things to their bodies.

Why? Because they believe that by performing physical actions
 they will find Nirvana.

Actions do not equal Nirvana.

Performing an action to obtain Nirvana is no different than the
person who believes that once they obtain a desired goal they will
never desire anything else. But as soon as they get it, they become
bored and move on to their next desire.

Physical action will not lead you to Nirvana.

Be Nirvana, and no external action or technique is necessary.

four

The concept of Goal Setting is claimed by many to be a necessary element to a fulfilled life.

Monks have claimed Nirvana as their goal for centuries.

Goals are fine but they create an atmosphere which is absent from fulfillment.

Every goal, even that of enlightenment, keeps you from Nirvana.

Why? Because when you believe you should have something you do not currently possess, no matter how seemingly holy, you keep yourself from witnessing the glory and perfection of your life in this moment.

Let go of goals and Nirvana is.

five

All life is movement.
Every element of this universe is in constant motion.

From science we learn that everything around us, from the smallest
subatomic particle to the largest planet, is in a state of continual flux.
The majority of this movement is unseen by the human eye.

All of this movement is in perfect harmony.

If it were not in perfect harmony, this place we call life would instantly
cease to exist.

If everything is moving in harmony, you too must be moving and
progressing in an unseen accord.

By understanding the Universe is in a harmony of movement—
this allows you to know that everything which takes place happens
for a reason. Thus, everything which occurs lends a hand in the
ever-expanding perfection of the Universe.

As you are a functioning part of this cosmic whole, everything which happens to you, no matter how seemingly traumatic, must be happening pursuant to a higher purpose and leading to a greater good.

Nirvana is acceptance. Relax, be peaceful, and watch the perfection of enlightenment unfold.

six

It is common for a devotee of a particular faith or school of thought to believe that the teachings they follow are the most profound and holy, and will lead its practitioners to self-realization in the most expedient fashion possible.

Nirvana is faithless.

seven

People enter onto the Spiritual Path for an untold number of reasons. Once this inclination strikes, they often times join a particular religious group. Those who remain involved within a specific sect, through time, come to gain prominence, respect, high ranking, and develop a strong voice within their denomination.

Prominence, respect, high ranking, and a loud voice does not constitute enlightenment.

Nirvana is unnoticed and silent.

eight

Nirvana is believed by many to be salvation.

Why do you need saving?

If you were saved — what would be different?

nine

People seek salvation because they are experiencing emptiness in their lives. This emptiness can take the form of lack of love, lack of purpose, lack of fulfillment, and so on.

In Zen — emptiness is sought after.

ten

Sunyata is the Sanskrit word which describes *Spiritual Voidness*—
the state beyond conceptual reality.

Sunyata is known to be the stepping stone to Nirvana.

The moment *Sunyata* becomes a desire in the mind of the zealot,
however, and techniques are designed for its obtainment, its true
spiritual purpose is lost.

Desires and techniques, in all cases, keep you from Nirvana. Because
they bind you to the doing, not the undoing.

Let go of desires.
Forget techniques.
Embrace Spiritual Voidness.
Know Nirvana.

eleven

When people enter onto the Spiritual Path, they oftentimes become very judgmental about other people who are not so inclined or who follow a different teaching.

They believe they are somehow more.

The moment this thought occurs—more becomes less.

We all are who we are—each person serves their own universal purpose.

Simply by considering yourself to be on the Spiritual Path does not give you a ticket to judge others.

All people are as important to this cosmic drama as you are.

No one is more or less.

The moment you think that you know—tells you that you do not know.

Experience, but be silent.
Know, but say nothing.
This is the true essence of Zen.

twelve

When people enter onto the Spiritual Path they generally seek guidance from a higher power. They often times go to a *Guru* or Spiritual Teacher in order to be directed down the road to Nirvana.

If we all are human beings and we all possess the Buddha nature. What does one person possess that another person does not?

What makes one person more than the next?

Is it simply because they have disciples?

How many people, throughout history, have claimed to hold the keys to Nirvana only to be later revealed as a fake?

If somebody claims to hold the key to Nirvana—
ask them to give it to you right away.

thirteen

You can listen to what other people have said about Nirvana.
You can worship them as being great knowers.
But, as long as that is all you do, you are not on the path to
Self-Realization, you are only on the path to being a devotee.

*Realization can only come when you stop being a disciple and start
being a personal realizer.*

fourteen

People who seek enlightenment oftentimes turn to the teaching of
Ancient Masters, believing that they were the only ones to teach the true
Dharma.

The stories of enlightened accomplishments of these Ancient Masters
are easy to tell. These people are no longer in their physical bodies.
Thus, their mastery can not be observed.

The written word is easier to follow, when you do not know the faults
of the author and do not have to look them in the face.

fifteen

Because Nirvana is an abstract concept, people are allowed to attach all types of metaphysical qualities to its obtainment.

"After achieving Nirvana this saint could perform the miracles of controlling the minds of other people and changing the flow of the river."

If somebody could do this—so what?

Does that make the world a better place?

Is Nirvana about the achievement of paranormal powers or is Nirvana about coming to embrace universal wholeness?

sixteen

There are many who vainly claim that they are fully enlightened and state that they are above the constraints of this physical existence.

Next time you meet one of these people,
spill a glass of water on them.

Is their cup half full
or half empty?

seventeen

When the Buddha was asked, "Are you a God?"
He answered, "No, simply a man."
"Then are you a Guru?"
"No, simply a man."

eighteen

The spiritual path is not a thermometer.

Spirituality is not gaged in the linear, higher or lower.

We all just are—each serving our own purpose.

The higher you get, the more you will realize this.

nineteen

Throughout the centuries the holy have walked upon the
Spiritual Path embracing nature as *Buddha Ksetra*, "The Buddha Realm."
They have believed that by living close to nature, Nirvana was close at hand.

Nature is soft in its appearance.
Nature is calm in its expressions.
Nature promises peace and serenity.

Beauty is readily witnessed in nature.
Meditation occurs with ease in nature.

Nirvana, however, is beyond the stimulation of the physical world.
Nirvana is not dominated by the serenity, or lack thereof, present in
any given environment.

Can you only be enlightened in nature?
No, enlightenment is everywhere.

twenty

Renunciation—for thousands of years people have renounced their worldly possessions, attempting to free themselves from the constraints of the material world in order that they may truly enter onto the spiritual path.

What are possessions?
Temporary physical objects—which, like human life, only last as long as they last.

You can give them up if you want to.
But does giving them up make you more holy?
No.
Giving them up only makes you someone who has given them up.

Nirvana does not come from releasing your hold on physical objects, which simply go back into the energy circulation of the material world.

Nirvana comes from not caring one way or the other about material possessions.

twenty-one

Your needs are your choice.

Because they are a choice, this means you are not bound by them.

You can choose to change your needs.

With no needs — Nirvana is known.

twenty–two

Ecstasy is not Nirvana.

Ecstasy is emotion pushed to its maximum level.

Ecstasy creates desire for a reoccurrence of the experience.

That desire for ecstasy creates the lack of Nirvana.

twenty-three

A *Koan* (a short Zen-based statement) speaks the ultimate reality.

Why? Because it says nothing.

"The moment in this vision is nothing to be stared at."

twenty-four

Zen is an abstract pathway towards realization.

Yet, countless Zen Doctrines have been written about how the individual must practice this, and perform that to obtain Nirvana.

Though many of the tenets are similar—many are also different.

Shouldn't the pathway to Nirvana be the same?
Shouldn't what one person says about Nirvana
be no different from the next?

Why are there differences?
Because the people who wrote the doctrines don't know.

They are only expanding the illusion about Nirvana—making it something impossible to obtain.

Nirvana is easy.

It is following all the paths to Nirvana which is difficult.

twenty-five

People become distracted from experiencing Nirvana by the
intensity of everyday life.

Jobs to go to because of bills to pay.
Concessions to make because of relationships.

If only you could be somewhere else, doing something else—
in a place where you could just be free, doing what you like...

Does doing what you like equal enlightenment?

No, Nirvana is where you are,
doing what you are doing.

twenty-six

Stop.
Go outside.
Take a walk down the busiest street you know.
Forgive.
Accept.
See love everywhere.
View the perfection of the nonstop interwoven components of this very
unique and interesting world.

This world is perfect—if you see it as perfect.

All of your actions, all of your emotions are perfect.
All of the actions and emotions of others are also perfect—even if you
choose not to like them.
Everything is perfect and in divine harmony with the universe.

See perfection as you encounter the world.
Accept perfection and Nirvana is on every corner.

twenty–seven

People commonly assume that if they could only become enlightened everything in their lives would change.

If you obtained Nirvana, what would be different?

Would you no longer need to eat, drink, or sleep?
Would you no longer need a place to live?
Would you no longer need money or a means to provide things for your physical body?

Nirvana equals change—yes.
But life is life—a human body is a human body.

Remember the old Zen saying,
"Before enlightenment—chop wood, carry water.
After enlightenment—chop wood, carry water."

twenty-eight

The Sanskrit word *Maya* is used to describe illusion.
This understanding details that all of life,
    all of this world, is illusion—it does not really exist.
    It is simply a projection of our deluded minds.

But, then what is life?
Why do we believe that we exist?

Some say this gives us the chance to regain the understanding
that we are, in fact, enlightened.

But why bother if we already are?

Maya additionally details that you not realizing you are already
enlightened is also illusion.

Maya is a concept.
Life is life.

The ultimate illusion is that there is no illusion.

Be Nirvana and Maya *becomes your friend.*

twenty-nine

What is an understanding?

Something which is accepted by more than one person.

A lot of people have accepted a lot of things—believed them to be truths, only to find out through time and experience that what they believed was, in fact, false.

Just because people have claimed an ideal to be true, does not make it true. No matter how ancient the understanding is proclaimed to be.

Truth is what you experience to be true.

thirty

All of your perceptions are defined by an untold list of parameters:

     your culture,
     your economic status,
     your previous experiences,
     your emotional state in a given moment,
     and the condition of world politics, to name a few.

Perceptions are not truth. They are only perceptions.

Truth lives beyond the temporary.
Truth exists in the realm beyond the thinking mind.

Let go and know the truth.

thirty-one

Each person's reality is different.

Though you may be living in the same world, same country, same city, even the same house or same room as another person — their life experience is different from yours. They have known different life defining events.

They are who they are.
You are who you are.

With this understanding, is Nirvana the same for each individual?
Or is it experienced by each person in their own way?

thirty-two

In meditation, the mind is trained to become one-pointed. With a one-pointed focus it can not be distracted. This one-pointedness is said to allow an individual to remove the veils of *Maya* and know Nirvana.

One-pointedness is nice. It gives you the ability to focus your attention precisely to accomplish worldly objectives.

Nirvana is not a worldly objective.

Nirvana is free from everything defined by the world.

thirty-three

Bodhidharma, the Indian monk who is credited with laying the foundation for modern Zen, traveled to China to become Abbott of the Shongshan (Shaolin) Monastery at the request of his teacher Prajnatara in the sixth century C.E. He is said to have sat in meditation, staring at a wall, for nine years.

What does sitting in front of a wall for nine years provide — Enlightenment?

Nirvana is.

If you want to sit in front of a wall for nine years to realize this, please do so.

thirty-four

Do you like what you see?

If you do not—look somewhere else.

thirty–five

A spiritual seeker looks into the mirror and says,
 "No, I am unworthy."
A monk looks into the mirror and says,
 "No I am unworthy."
An ego-filled, young, attractive, successful, business person looks into
the mirror and says,
 "I am very worthy."

What is the difference?

From a worldly perspective, people believe they can have it all.

From a spiritual perspective, people are indoctrinated into believing that
spiritual experience is such a far off plateau that there is always more to
know, more to learn, more good deeds to perform before they can even
hope to have a glimpse of the absolute.

Nirvana is, Right Now, where are you?
Thinking about how unworthy you are?

thirty-six

Why have seekers of enlightenment, throughout the centuries, performed seemingly unnatural acts in order to gain insight, wisdom, and enlightenment?

Because to understand Nirvana, you need to step outside of the normality of everyday existence and rational thought.

By stepping outside of everyday existence, you enter a world of abstraction.

When you come to embrace the abstract—Nirvana is instantly realized.

thirty-seven

Many of life's ongoing experiences become accepted discomfort.

When you were a child and you did not like something, most likely you expressed your discontent by crying.

As you grow up, you learn to temper your feelings and accept situations you do not particularly feel comfortable in: jobs, living conditions, dysfunctional relationships, and the like.

If you relate this understanding to the average person, they will simply tell you, "That's Life" or "You've grown up."

But, is that what life is about — acceptance of discomfort?

Many people personally direct their bodies into discomfort by working out in a gym or sitting for untold hours in meditation.

Is this truly a pathway to a healthier body and a more enlightened mind?

If you step outside of what is expected of you,
if you move beyond what society has guided you to do,
you will find a completely different world—defined by a
completely new set of rules—a place where there are no rules.

No rules = Nirvana.

thirty-eight

Sometimes your cup is full.
Sometimes it is empty.

*What do you do differently when it is full as opposed to
when it is empty?*

thirty-nine

The root cause of unhappiness is desire.

Desire for things that you want,
desire for people that you want,
desire for things to be more, less, or different than they are.

Desire is desire.

It is so simple — let go of desire and you are free.

Free — Nirvana can be seen.

forty

If you focus upon what isn't in your life, then you will find that
you are continually lacking something:

be it position,
love,
money,
or enlightenment.

Let life happen as it happens.

Know and accept the fullness of each moment.

Look around yourself, see everything as if you have never seen
it before.

When life is new, your understandings are new.

Nirvana is, when Nirvana is.

forty-one

Internal peace is a choice.

The world will give you a million reasons to not be peaceful if you allow external images and negative stimuli to dominate your emotions.

Next time you find yourself upset—stop everything.

Be still.
Let your mind rest.
Do not let momentary emotions control you.
Catch them and watch them fly away like a beautiful bird across a scenic horizon.
Understand that whoever or whatever has led you to this unpeaceful state is not worthy of controlling your life.

Allow yourself to feel peace—even in the most unpeaceful events and enlightenment will be yours.

forty-two

Nature is silent in its own perfection.
The city pounds with nonstop intensity.
You are where you are.

Silence your mind in the pounding intensity and you will know Nirvana.

forty-three

If all of the enlightened masters say that obtaining Nirvana is easy, then why doesn't the whole world know Nirvana?

Because the concept of Nirvana keeps people from understanding its simplicity.

People read books, hear stories, and believe they know what Nirvana must be like.

Tales told—are not experiences known.

Nirvana can not be described.

Forget everything you know and you will know Nirvana.

forty-four

Self–Actualization is not Self–Realization.

A Self–Actualized individual focuses on what their needs are, how to systematically obtain them, and how each individual should interact with one another.

A Self-Realized individual understands that needs and proper interactions are only as temporary as this physical existence. Thus, overtly seeking them keeps one from Nirvana.

forty-five

Siddhartha Guatama, the Sakyamuni Buddha, upon seeing poverty, illness, and death for the first time, left his wife, newborn child, and royal lifestyle to go on a quest to understand the meaning of life. He traveled India for seven years as a *Sadhu* (wandering holy man), studying spiritual traditions in hopes of unveiling the truth.

Frustrated by not finding the ultimate meaning of life he sat down under a Bodhi Tree, in Bodh Gaya, India, and swore he would not get up until he obtained realization. Thirty days later he rose an enlightened being.

How many people over the centuries have attempted to do what the Buddha did—sit, lost deeply in meditation and obtain realization?

How many people have sat for days, weeks, months, even years and have not experienced enlightenment?

The road to Nirvana is different for each individual.
Chart you own path.

forty-six

Siddhartha Guatama studied with two primary *Gurus* on his quest towards Nirvana.

Arada Kalama taught him *Akimcanya Ayatana*,
"The experience of nothingness."

Udraka Ramaputra taught him *Naiva Samjna Asamjna Ayatana*,
"The experience of conscious unconsciousness."

Siddhartha realized flaws in both of these teachings.

He sat down, realized his own enlightenment, and emerged a Buddha.

His teachers' enlightenment were not his.
His enlightenment was not theirs.

Is one individual's enlightenment more valid that someone else's?

forty–seven

The Buddha did not invent meditation.
He did not create the concept of Nirvana.

Through his efforts, he embraced Transcendental Consciousness
and spoke about his realizations.

Each individual is unique.
No one else's realizations can be your realization.

If you attempt to imitate the Buddha's understandings,
you will not find Nirvana.

Nirvana is only known when you personally interact
with Cosmic Consciousness.

forty-eight

The word Buddha comes from the Sanskrit root *Budh,*
which means, "to awaken."

In the Pali Canons of Buddhism it is recorded that there were twenty-eight Buddhas or enlightened beings who existed before Siddhartha Guatama.

Twenty-eight before, how many afterwards?

Enlightenment is available.

forty-nine

The Sakyamuni Buddha taught The Four Noble Truths:

1. All beings are bound by Karma.
2. The cause of suffering is desire.
3. Suffering can be alleviated by obtaining enlightenment.
4. Enlightenment is obtainable by practicing the Eightfold Path of Dharma:

    1. Right Views.
    2. Right Intentions.
    3. Right Speech.
    4. Right Conduct.
    5. Right Livelihood.
    6. Right Effort.
    7. Right Mindfulness.
    8. Right Concentration.

    OK. . .

fifty

How many Buddhists have lost themselves in practicing
the Four Noble Truths and the Eightfold Path?

How many Buddhists have embraced guilt instead of Nirvana because
their minds have swayed from the precepts of these teachings and they
believed themselves unworthy?

Did the Buddha teach desire and guilt
or did he teach a path to Nirvana?

fifty-one

Teachings are the understanding of one individual.

Teachings are a guideline laid down by someone who has traveled a path before you.

Teachings are good, but teachings are not enlightenment; they are only the realizations of another individual.

Embrace Nirvana and all teachings can be forgotten.

fifty-two

The Buddha taught universal oneness.

Was the Buddha the same as his disciples?

No, he was not.

He was their teacher.

What makes the difference between a teacher and his students?

When the student knows the answer to this question,
a teacher is no longer needed,
and oneness is embraced.

Whose fault is it that you are not enlightened—your teacher's?

fifty-three

If you allow yourself to embrace a state of mind where other people make you happy or sad, you hold yourself bound to the illusion that happiness is something external to yourself.

Outside is always outside.
Another person may make you happy,
      but they are not you.
They desire what they desire.
For a time, they may desire to make you happy
      and offer you fulfillment.
What happens when they overcome this desire?

Internal happiness is born where you become you.
It does not come from the external stimulation of another individual providing you with some abstract stimuli.

Naturally happy, you do not seek experiences outside of yourself.
Not focusing on the external world, True Self is revealed.
True Self is the passageway to Nirvana.

fifty-four

The word *Zazen* means, "to sit in Zen."

This is the term which is commonly used to describe formal seated meditation.

Sit down, cross your legs. Focus your half closed eyes on a spot on the floor approximately three feet in front of you.

With each in-breath, count the number, "One."
With each out-breath, count the number, "Two."
"One, Two," "One, Two," "One, Two."

Do not let yourself think.
When a thought comes to your mind,
watch it fly away like a beautiful bird on a scenic horizon.

Refocus,
"One, Two," "One, Two," "One, Two."

fifty-five

Meditation is good.
From meditation you develop a calm and focused mind.

With a calm and focused mind,
you possess a calm and focused mind.

Is a calm and focused mind the experience of Nirvana?

No, a calm and focused mind is simply a calm and focused mind.

fifty-six

People sit in *Zazen* for all of the wrong reasons.
They sit for results — enlightenment.
They sit for experience — cosmic visions.
They sit for ego — "I can sit without moving longer than you can."
They sit for conversation — "I have meditated for so long,
  I am finally embracing the truths which are spoken of
  in the scriptures."
They sit to be seen as holy — all the great sages meditated,
  didn't they?

Zazen is not about knowing.
Zazen is not about achieving.
Zazen is not about talking.
Zazen is not about being holy.
Zazen is not about doing.
Zazen is about undoing.

If you want to practice *Zazen*,
don't seek,
don't discuss,
and mostly don't think.
Because thinking makes you want to be something more than the essence
of egoless simplicity which Zazen is designed to embrace.

Think and be.
Don't think and "Sit in Zen."

fifty-seven

In meditation, people close their eyes.

They believe that to meditate they must isolate themselves from the external world.

Does sitting in meditation for a few minutes or even several hours a day give you Nirvana?

Isn't Nirvana the embracing of all things, not the running away from anything?

fifty-eight

The meditator is trained to think of nothing.

The thought of no thought is still a thought.

fifty-nine

Meditation separates your from enlightenment.
Why?
Because meditation makes you think that you are doing something
which will equal something—realization.

Doing something never equals Nirvana.
Nirvana is only known in the non-doing.

This is the greatest illusion of meditation.
Trapping you in "The doing,"
Keeping you from "The undoing."

Undo.

sixty

Rocks sit quietly and do not move.

Is a rock enlightened?

sixty-one

Nirvana is not gained by teaching your body to sit for long periods of time in some uncomfortable meditation posture. That practice only teaches you discipline.

Physical and mental discipline is good, because it allows you to maintain precise control over your material, tangible life. But physical and mental discipline does not equal Nirvana, only a disciplined body and mind.

Nirvana comes naturally.

Allow it to enter you from where you are—Right Now.

sixty-two

A person sits down to meditate and becomes frustrated because they can not stop their thoughts.

They are certain that everyone around them is obviously much more holy —lost deeply in meditation.

Meditation is designed to calm your mind, not make it more disrupted.

Relax into your own being.
Be who you are.
Be what you are.

Allow your mind to be silent
and you will not need to chase this silence in formal meditation.

Zen is about being, not becoming.

sixty-three

A lover keeps his attention tightly locked onto his partner.
A musician keeps his attention tightly locked onto his instrument.
A surfer keeps his attention tightly locked onto the wave.
A physicist keeps his attention tightly locked onto his calculations.
A scientist keeps his attention tightly locked onto his experiment.

How locked is your attention on Cosmic Consciousness?

sixty–four

Life becomes a nonstop series of habitual reenactments
of previous experiences.

Why?
Because they are known.
Known—nothing is new.
With nothing new, no uncharted emotions or experiences
must take place.

Meditation is a habitual experience.
As a habitual experience, after the initial stages of its mental focusing have
been achieved, nothing new is gained from it.

This is the reason that people meditate for a lifetime but do not achieve
realization—they lock themselves into the limited experience which they
have mastered.

Meditation does not have to be habitual.
It can be new each time you sit.

Do you allow it to be new?
Do you allow yourself to encounter new experiences behind
the walls of meditation?

Life is your choice.
Meditation is your choice.
Do with it what you will.

sixty-five

Nirvana is not an "I" subject.

This is why so many people throughout the centuries have sought after it but have not obtained its bliss.

You can not want Nirvana.
That is desire.

You can not choose to pursue Nirvana.
That is working towards the unobtainable.

You can not deserve Nirvana.
That is egotism.

You can not demand Nirvana.
That is lust.

Nirvana is, when you are not.

Cease to be and become Nirvana.

sixty-six

Can you think your way to Nirvana?

sixty–seven

"You" can never reach Nirvana.
Because "You" is a concept of your Thinking Mind.

The Thinking Mind thinks.
The Thinking Mind is the illustrator of illusion.

Stop thinking about Nirvana.
And Nirvana is yours.

sixty-eight

What are you?
Are you your body which becomes old and eventually dies?

Are you your thinking mind which is driven by ever-changing emotions and desires?

Perhaps you are a soul, hidden deep beneath all of the external images and desires?

Or, a spark of pure spiritual energy which you have not yet encountered?

If you are, how do you know?

Simply because someone else has told you that a ethereal being exists within you, does not mean that it is true.

As long as you look to your "I"
understanding is always in question.

Look beyond "I" and know Nirvana.

sixty-nine

All of this Universe,
from the smallest subatomic particle
to the largest planet is vibrating with an energy.
You too are pulsating with this energy.

The ancient Yogis gave this energy the name, *"Prana."*
The ancient Chinese called it, *"Chi."*

Look around yourself,
experience the energy pulsation in everything which makes up
your field of vision.

Look to the movement of the clouds,
the touch of the unseen wind,
the embrace of the raindrop,
the glow of the sun,
the illumination of a lightbulb,
the movement of the passing car.

Everything, man-made or otherwise,
pulsates with this unseen energy.

Lose your individual pulsation.
Join the universal vibration.
Meet Nirvana.

seventy

STOP!
Right now, right where you are.
Don't think about stopping—just STOP!

Look around yourself.
See everything as if you are encountering it for the first time.

Take this moment and truly study the physical objects around you,
even if you know you have seen them a thousand times before.

Let go of your knowing and realize the profound beauty of even
the most mundane article of this physical existence.

From this simple exercise you will begin to reeducate yourself
to the amazing beauty of the Here and Now.

You will be amazed at your realizations.

seventy-one

Many people believe that they have something special and unique
to offer the world.

If they could only get away from the daily grind of their jobs
and family obligations they would be able to give it to the world.

Life is life.
It is a perfect interaction of energies and relationships.

You are offering the world something very important and unique
right now—because you are doing what you are doing.

By doing what you are doing, the world is functioning in its perfection.

Embrace the perfection.
Let go of the desires.
And offering the world something special—naturally occurs.

seventy-two

To the worldly masses, Nirvana is a joke.
To the enlightened, Nirvana is also a joke.

Same concept—different point of view.
Think about it...

seventy-three

Religious people look at bad times as a test
and good times as a gift.

If you let go of desire
you will not differentiate good from bad,
because you will understand that it is all a point of view.

How can bad times be a test when you love them?
How can good times be a gift when you love it with
the same intensity as you do the bad times?

Let your life become simple.
See all situations as simply unique occurrences
on your pathway towards Nirvana.

seventy-four

Prayer equals desire.

No desire.
Praying is not necessary.

seventy–five

Religious people love to argue about the validity of their religion, sect, teacher, and teaching—claiming that it is the best and the only path to Pure Consciousness.

The enlightened do not argue.
Because the enlightened have nothing to prove.

Thus, the enlightened are not religious people.

seventy-six

The sage desires
no wealth,
no power,
no fame,
no love,
no enlightenment.

Desire-less, Nirvana rushes towards him.

seventy-seven

The Japanese word *Ku* means "Emptiness."

The understanding of *Ku* teaches:
If you think you know, you never know.

Ku *is the foundation for Nirvana.*

seventy-eight

Ku can not be understood.
Ku can not be defined.
There are no workable techniques
which will cause you to embrace *Ku*.
So, what is *Ku*?

Ku is abstract like Zen is abstract.
Ku is undefined like the wind.
Ku can not be touched.
Ku can not be known.
Yet, *Ku* is the essence of Nirvana.

Let go of your thoughts.
Let go of your understandings.
Let go of your definitions.
Embrace the divine void.
And Ku *will become you.*

seventy-nine

Ku is the essential element to Zen.
Ku separates you from the way you think things are supposed to be.

You can think about Nirvana.
You can imagine what it is like.
You can attempt to put a definition on Nirvana.
But if you think Nirvana, you do not know Nirvana.

Ku is thoughtlessness.

Thoughtless, you are Nirvana.

eighty

The majority of the world's population travels through their lives in a state of unconsciousness. They pass from birth to death, moving from one temporal emotion to the next, driven by desire. When their life has past, they ask, "Where did it go?"

Ku is not unconsciousness.
Ku is profound consciousness,
     obtained by consciously encountering Spiritual Emptiness.

What is Spiritual Emptiness?

The letting go of faith.

Why must you relinquish faith?
Because faith holds you bound to belief.
Belief is something you think that you know.

Thinking has nothing to do with Zen.

Zen is the embracing of No-Thought.
No-Thought is where you meet Nirvana.

eighty-one

To consciously become nothing
is very different from ending up as nothing.

A worldly person chases wealth, power, status,
and even illumination.

When they do not achieve it,
they despise all of humanity and blame Karma and God.

What if they never choose to pursue anything?

If they desired nothing,
who would they need to blame for not achieving it?

Exist.
Be.
And, you are.

When you are,
Nirvana is.

eighty-two

Thoughts give birth to emotions.
Emotions give birth to desire.
Desire gives birth to actions.
Actions give birth to Karma.

> Karma, the law of cause and effect:
> *as you sow, so shall you reap.*

Ku sets you free from Karma
which was given birth by actions,
which was born from desires,
which were based in emotions.

Let go.
Know Ku.

eighty-three

We are trained from birth to encounter the world, thought, emotions, and feelings.

Personality and culture provides us with a set of standards.

Do you like it?
How do you feel?

Emotions are not Zen.
Feelings are not Nirvana.

eighty-four

Some parents who have been exposed to higher consciousness attempt
to pass their understanding on to their children.
But understanding can not be passed on.
Understanding can only be personally realized.

When you think you know, you do not know.
When you attempt to teach what you know to unwilling ears,
you really never know.

Ku *is unknowing what you know.*

eighty-five

You can be dominated by external circumstances
or you can BE.

If you allow yourself to be dominated by things outside of your control
you will forever be locked into desiring that things were different.

What is outside of your control?
Life.

What is under your control?
How you experience your life.

Choose.

eighty-six

People spend much of their life struggling to take control over the various factors which dominate their physical existence:

> where they live,
> how they live,
> who they live with.

Many believe that by mastering one or more of these external dominates they will somehow, some way gain a state of grace and never need to struggle to achieve anything again.

By believing this, they make internal peace and a life lived in the moment secondary to the nonstop pursuit of sought-after illusion.

As long as you focus your life on something external, even enlightenment, your life will forever be a battle.

A battle never equals peace.

External is never whole or complete.

Accepting the unlikely perfection of the external world can, however, make it whole and complete.

Let go and know.

eighty–seven

People make all kinds of excuses for doing what they are doing,
      no matter what the consequences to themselves or others.

Why?
Because the structure of the physical world allows this to take place.

"I have to earn money, don't I?"
"I need a place to live, don't I?"
"I can't be looked down upon by others, can I?"

These worldly motivating factors are simply justifications for doing what
you want to do at whatever cost—without any consideration for whom
you are negatively effecting by your actions.

How does your job effect the world around you?
How does what you are doing to achieve your desires effect
the energy of this universe?

If you can't consciously answer these questions,
how do you expect to meet Nirvana?

*Nirvana is never embraced in a state of moral justification
or psychological denial.*

eighty–eight

Karma is either good or bad.
There is no neutral karma.

Worldly motivations are the source point for Karma.

As long as you keep enhancing your Karma, whether it be good or bad, you can not meet Nirvana.

Why?
Because Karma holds you bound to the ways of the world.

Where there is action, there is reaction.
People can love you.
People can hate you.
In essence, it is the same thing.

If you are locked into an endless cycle of karma,
    whether your karma is good or bad,
actions only equal reactions.
This only equals that.
    Thus, the cycle will never be broken.
Stop.
Be.
Let go of the ways of the world.
Karma ends.
Nirvana is yours.

eighty-nine

Karma is the source point for a disrupted life.
A disrupted life keeps you from experiencing Nirvana.

"I have been bad, so I must suffer."

Thus, you guide yourself down a pathway where you bring negative experiences into your life and feel they are justified.

"I have been good, so I deserve good things to come to me."

When they don't, you feel you have been cheated.

Karma is not the pathway to Nirvana.
Karma is the pathway to justice.
Justice has nothing to do with enlightenment.
Justice has to do with culture, society, and a worldly outlook based in the judgment of good and bad.

Do good things but do not seek results.

Do not care and you are free.

Free, you instantly meet Nirvana.

ninety

Life happens.

The moment something seemingly negative occurs, people commonly focus all of their consciousness upon attempting to figure out what caused the occurrence.

How many times have you inquired, "Why me?"

It is common to turn to the concept of Karma for a justification.

"Did it happen because I did that, then?"
"Maybe when I acted this way to that person?"
Or, "Why, I don't deserve it!"

You can sit around attempting to figure out why.
You can question the justification for it.
Or, you can accept that life is life,
that something did happen,
and move on.

Which way do you think will lead you to enlightenment?

ninety-one

Thoughts equal ideas.
Ideas equal creations.
Creations cause things to happen.
Things happening equals Karma.

If you didn't have the thought which equaled the idea for the creation
of something you would not have set its implementation into motion.
Thus, people would not have been affected by it and you would not hold
the Karma of all those people who were exposed to it in your hands.

In Zen, everyday you step beyond thoughts.
With no thought, no new things are created.
With no new things created, there is no new Karma.
With no new Karma you are whole onto yourself.
Whole onto yourself, the universe is peaceful as it should be.

You don't have to create to BE.

ninety–two

People exchange their Present Moment Consciousness
for sensory gratification.

You can go after what you want and get it.
That is easy.

You can seek and find.
That is easy too.

You can say,
"I don't care about anything and I don't want anything or anybody,"
that is also easy.

Because all of these things are based in the realms of what you want for
whatever reason you desire it.

Letting go of what you want is the first step into understanding Zen.

Zen teaches *Mushin*, "No-Minded-ness."

No-Minded-ness is the only place where Nirvana is found.

ninety-three

Mushin no Shin, "Mind unconscious of itself."

Life teaches consciousness.
Zen teaches conscious unconsciousness.

The mind that believes itself to be conscious is, in fact,
the most unconscious.

It separates itself from the wholeness of interactive oneness.

Lock yourself into your mind
and you lock yourself into your ego.
Locked in an ego, you see life as hostile;
full of unfulfilled desires,
objects you can't possess,
people you can't control,
and deeds you must do,
because the ends justify the means.

Let go of all the justification nonsense.
Meet Zen.

ninety-four

Thoughts place obstacles in your path to realization.
Why?
Because thoughts are beliefs.
From beliefs come the concept of right and wrong.
From right and wrong comes conflict.

"I know. You do not."
"My way is right because the scriptures and my teacher say so.
That means your way is wrong."

Thoughts never lead to realization.
No thoughts, no conflict.
No conflict, the path to Nirvana is revealed.

ninety-five

Existing in *Mushin*, "No-Mind," you do not care if you are right
    or wrong.
You do not care what the scriptures or a teacher says.
You exist, thus you are.
Simply being, you embrace the perfection.

ninety–six

Ushin no Shin, "Mind conscious of itself."

With a conscious mind,
you want the things you want,
the way you want them.

You calculate,
you plan,
you devise a method for obtaining what you desire.

This is ego consciousness.
No matter how much modern society promises you will obtain from this
mindset, you will never be fulfilled, because the ego is not eternal. It is lost
to the bounds of temporary lust and desire.

With mind focused upon mind,
life loses its naturalness and spontaneity.
Without naturalness, the perfection of the universe is hidden,
as desires overrule the unexplained.

With your mind focused upon you,
you can never let go of you.
Holding on to you, you may get what you think you want,
but you will not find enlightenment.
Enlightenment can not be found in a mind focused upon itself.

Let go.

ninety-seven

The thinking mind can not understand No-Mind.
The thinking mind can talk about No-Mind.
The thinking mind can only attempt to describe No-mind.
But, No-Mind only exists in you.

Let go of the techniques and teachings
and No-Mind is surprisingly easy to encounter.

ninety-eight

In *Mushin*, there are no obstacles.
Why?
Because you allow everything to be as it is.
You do not resist the natural path of your human existence.

In *Mushin*, thoughts of yourself and what you desire are not allowed
to rob the perfection of this moment.

Mushin is easy.
Look deeply into yourself.
Define all of your desires.
When you begin to truly look at them you will experience how
truly meaningless they are.
Witness them leaving you,
naturally dissipating into the air.

With no desire, you do not care. You see how everything is perfect.
Witnessing perfection, you instantly know Mushin.

ninety-nine

You are born.
You live.
You die.

Your concept of self only exists in the interim between birth and death.

Thus, self is not eternal.

If self is temporary,
why do you place so much emphasis upon catering to its needs?

Let go of the temporariness and meet Nirvana.

one hundred

As long as you are on the Spiritual Path you have not met Nirvana.

A path is simply a roadway.
It guides you in a direction.

A path takes you, but it is you who must arrive.

Are you on the Spiritual Path
Or, are you encountering Nirvana?

one hundred one

There is confrontation everywhere if you seek confrontation.
There are those who want to beat you, defeat you, out-maneuver you,
and even become you.

To do this, they will go to all lengths to succeed in their victory.

If you fight, they have already won,
because they drew you into the battle.

If you compete, they have already won, because you have lowered yourself
to a world defined by winners and losers.

No winners,
no losers,
no Karma.

Walk away.

one hundred two

If you win a battle what have you won?
If you engage in confrontation and defeat your adversary who has
really lost?

Battles are only as temporary as the people who wage them.
Battles create loss.
> Loss of loved ones,
> loss of honor,
> loss of the way things were.

How does a battle equal justice, when so many people suffer?

Acceptance equals no battles.

No battles is Zen.

one hundred three

The world around you may be:
confrontational,
competitive,
desirous,
even violent,
but it is your choice if you enter into this folly.

Sit in the presence of the unenlightened,
let them fight their battles.
Do not become involved,
and they will turn to you for peace.
When they do,
say nothing, do nothing,
for with nothing given, nothing need be returned.

They will learn from your silence and simply become like you — quiet.

Then the world will again be allowed to follow its own course of perfection.

one hundred four

Yin and Yang.

If you have to think about whether or not you are in balance,
you are out of balance.

Balance is the state of oneness.
An understanding of your integral interrelationship
with the cosmic whole.

What sets a person out of balance?
Not understanding that balance is the natural order of things.
This causes striving for realignment.

Striving, in all cases, sets in motion the causation factors
for human suffering.

Be
and you are.
Try
and you are not.

one hundred five

Yin and Yang defines duality.

I am this,
you are that.

I am right,
you are wrong.

I am man,
you are woman.

I am white,
you are black.

Duality causes life.
Duality causes Karma.
Duality does not cause enlightenment.

Step beyond duality.
See yourself as an interactive part of everything.
Let your mind merge with the oneness.
And you will be free from Karma.

one hundred six

If you love Hell
it becomes Heaven.

Good and bad
are all your perspective, your point of view.

If good and bad, right or wrong are based in the individual,
it is only your individuality you must transcend to meet Nirvana.

Become one.

one hundred seven

Everybody wants to go to Heaven
but nobody wants to die.

People want to be holy,
but only if the world knows that they are holy.
So they wear certain clothing or hold a specific title.

Holiness comes with a price, no Nirvana.

Enlightenment also comes with a price, your ego.

As long as you prefer holiness over enlightenment,
Nirvana can not be known.

How do you let go of the desire for holiness?
Step One:
Don't care if anyone knows you're enlightened.

one hundred eight

If you promise to meditate at the same time everyday,
for a specific length of time,
with the hopes of obtaining enlightenment,
you will never encounter illumination.

Nirvana doesn't know what time it is.

one hundred nine

The door to liberation is wide open.

You can not see that it is wide open because you think you know how
you are supposed to feel and act when you come upon it.

Why?
Because those who posses the title of "Enlightened" have lied to you.

Does an enlightened person claim they are enlightened?
If they do, they are not.

Since they are not,
how can they tell you what enlightenment is?

Zen is.
You are.
Stop believing.
Start experiencing.

one hundred ten

Books,
Lectures,
and Classes
lead to understanding.

Understanding leads to knowledge.

Knowledge is not enlightenment.

Knowledge is,
"I know.
You don't.
Let me teach you."

Understanding illusion is easy.

Nobody can teach you Nirvana.

Nirvana knows nothing.
It exists beyond teachings.

one hundred eleven

People who don't understand use the Thinking Mind to attempt
to teach No-Mind.

They lay down elaborate techniques for you to find your way
to nothingness.

They initiate you with secret *Mantras* so you will have a focus
of meditation.

They tell you to sit, thinking nothing but the *Mantra*
and you will meet Nirvana.

But from techniques comes evaluation.
From evaluation comes judgment.
From judgment rank is born.
From rank comes title.
From title comes superiority.
From superiority comes ego.
From ego comes illusion.

Techniques are not the pathway to Nirvana.
Techniques are only the pathway to illusion.

How long can you sit without having a thought?

If you answer this,
you are only focused on the quality of your technique.

one hundred twelve

Some people want to be disciples.

They need to believe that some other human being knows
more than they do.

There is a certain assurance in the fact that you do not have
all the answers.

But what are the answers?
Aren't they simply individual perceptions of the cosmic interplay?

When somebody says they know,
they only know what they know.

What do you know?
You probably know more than you think you know.

one hundred thirteen

The world provides us with tons of Mind Stuff.
The need to be:
bigger,
better,
stronger,
thinner,
smarter,
richer,
more attractive.

Zen provides us with tons of Mind Stuff.
The need to be:
purer,
less materialistic,
less desirous,
more meditative,
more enlightened.

Mind Stuff is Mind Stuff.
Nirvana is beyond Mind Stuff.

Does the average person ever question who they are or why they are the way they are?

In Zen, it is taught that the simplest is the purist. Yet the unenlightened Zen teacher takes away simplicity and replaces it with the illusion of Mind Stuff.

Nirvana is free from Mind Stuff.
Even that Mind Stuff provided by Zen.

one hundred fourteen

Consciousness is the simplest science.

Yet, due to the abstract nature of consciousness, it is the hardest science to define.

Because consciousness is so abstract, people can say anything they want about it and find somebody to believe them.

Is belief enlightenment?
No, enlightenment is you letting go of belief,
stepping into your own consciousness,
and emerging with your own cosmic understanding.

one hundred fifteen

There is beauty in the flight of a bird.
There is grace in the animals who stalk the forests.

But their essence is their essence,
they possess their own set of life parameters.

To look to them to find a pathway to enlightenment
robs the perfection of both human and animal consciousness.

Be what you are.
Love your faults and limitations.
Accept your own innate perfection.
And enlightenment need be sought nowhere else.

one hundred sixteen

Can a drug provide you with enlightenment?

A drug may make you feel good.
A drug may give you new experiences.
A drug may even cause you to see visions that you believe to be real.

What is real?
Is real not what is real?

If a drug could give you enlightenment, why do the effects of a drug fade away—leaving you only with the memory of the experience?

Nirvana is,
without anything else.

one hundred seventeen

What if Nirvana came in a box.
Would you open it?

one hundred eighteen

Absent Reality.

How many times have you been driving to some location, only to realize that you do not remember traveling the last several miles?

How many times have you eaten a meal, never tasting a bite?

How many times have you become aware, in the middle of an experience, and realized you are living it but not truly experiencing it?

Due to the onslaught of the modern world, many people have unconsciously come to block out how their bodies and minds truly experience anything in any given moment. This leads to a life lived without an interaction with self.

Without the interaction of self, life passes by in a blur, and realizations are left to those who wish to touch their moment.

one hundred nineteen

Awareness.

How do you feel?
Saying "I feel fine," is not an answer.
How do you really feel right now?
Let your mind study each element of your physical being:
your toes, feet, legs, fingers, arms, torso, neck and head.
Once you have accessed your physical components, turn your
attention to your inner being.
Take a long hard, non-critical, look at yourself. Experience who you are.

No one can tell you how to feel.
There is no right and wrong.
Your experience of you is your experience of you.

If you don't know you,
you can not know Nirvana.

Meet yourself intimately, for the first time.

one hundred twenty

Enlightenment is not based in denial.
Enlightenment is not based in pretend.
Enlightenment is not wanting to be something you are not.
Enlightenment is not something you hope to be someday.

Enlightenment is yours, Now.
Get into this moment and experience it.

one hundred twenty-one

If you want an answer to a question,
you can find someone to give it to you.
But, an answer means different things to different people,
based on individual perception.

Perception leads to illusion.
For there is no universal truth in a world which is defined by
the limitations of logical understanding.

If you don't seek answers you will not be lied to.
Not lied to, you are free from deception.
Free from deception, you can encounter life on your own terms.

Understanding yourself, you see the world clearly.
As it is only you who is viewing it.

Seeking no answers, is your pathway to Nirvana.

one hundred twenty-two

There is a Source Point for everything:
the universe,
physical existence,
human problems,
desires,
even enlightenment.

Finding the Source Point is the key to enlightenment.

The Source Point is obtained by removing obstructions.

Obstructions are caused by society, culture, religion, science,
and your desires.

Why? Because people desire an answer.
But, there are no answers.
What is religiously or scientifically right today,
    will be wrong tomorrow.
What is desired today, will be forgotten tomorrow.

Strip away obstructions.
Seek the Source Point.
You will find the door to illumination.

one hundred twenty-three

One of the key factors which keeps you from Nirvana
is fixation upon a specific emotion — be it positive or negative.

Emotions are addictive.
They make you feel.
Feelings makes your adrenalin pump,
which provides you with the enhanced sense of being alive.

But emotions don't last forever.
By their very nature they come and then they go.

Emotions lead to emotions, lead to emotions, lead to emotions.

How emotional are you?
Are you dominated by your emotions?
How will your emotions direct you to Nirvana?

one hundred twenty-four

An emotion is a drug.

Once experienced, you either desire to frequently encounter it
or seek to never feel that way again.

You set your life into a pattern of either encountering or running away
from a specific emotion.

Emotions are not Nirvana.
Emotions are only feelings.
And, feelings pass.

Illumination never fades away.

Your choice,
pursue a lifetime of emotions or know Nirvana.

one hundred twenty-five

Why are you angry?

Because you are not getting what you want?
Because someone is not behaving in the fashion you desire?

You can be angry if you want to.
But what does anger lead to?
Anger leads to confrontation, poor health, and unhappiness.
It does not lead to enlightenment.

What do you do with anger?
Realize that it is born in desire—desire for something
to be different.

If you are in your moment,
embracing the perfection,
anger can never grab you.

one hundred twenty-six

Zen is not about the repression of your emotions.
Zen is about realization.

Enlightenment is not about running away from your emotions.
Enlightenment is about embracing the source of everything,
including your emotions.

Embracing the source,
you understand causation.

Understanding causation,
you are no longer unduly controlled by the temporariness
of your emotions.

Not controlled,
you are in control.
One step closer to Nirvana.

one hundred twenty-seven

You can embrace the common elements of human existence:
>momentary anger,
>temporary desires,
>seeking,
>longing,
>and emotions which lead you down untold paths of confusion,
>if you like.

Or, you can turn off the transient nature of everyday human life and know Nirvana.

Your life — your choice.

one hundred twenty-eight

People assume that enlightenment means happiness.

Happiness feels good.
Happiness feels better than being sad.
But, happiness is an emotion.
Emotions do not last forever.
They come and they go, motivated by external circumstance.

Enlightenment is beyond happiness,
because it is not motivated by anything.

It is full and complete unto itself.
Are you?

one hundred twenty-nine

If you embrace Cosmic Perfection —
understanding that everything is as it should be,
then you enter into what is known as,
"The Path of Least Resistance."

In this state of mind, you no longer fight with yourself
over your impurities.
You do not battle with the world over injustice.
You do what you do, that is the nature of life,
but you do not become lost in the results.
Not lost in the results, they are allowed to happen.
Allowed to happen, there is no conflict in you,
because you experience the perfection of each movement
of your life and that of the universe.
With no conflict,
everything is as it should be, including you.

Step into the Path of Least Resistance.

one hundred thirty

You can witness the occurrence of the physical world around you.
You can watch the actions of other human beings.
You can even sit back and observe your own Life Time pass by,
waiting for it to be over.
Or, you can embrace consciousness and become an active participant
of this divine melodrama.

Does running away to a cave promise enlightenment?
Does hiding from the world mean you will meet Nirvana?
Does living in denial that you are a human being with the frailties
of human existence promise illumination?

Let go of all the nonsensical beliefs propagated by those who
do not know.

Know and you know.
Be and you are.

one hundred thirty-one

The Japanese word, *Satori*,
      refers to "Instantaneous Enlightenment."

Coming from nothing
it goes to nothing.

It exists and then it is gone.
Perfect, like life.

Here—gone,
the cycle complete.

one hundred thirty–two

You can not hold onto *Satori*,
because there is nothing to grasp.

You can not define *Satori*,
because it is not a thing.

Not being anything,
it is the perfect expression of Zen.

one hundred thirty-three

You can remember the experience of *Satori*,
that is human nature.

But if you attempt to describe *Satori*,
its essence is lost.

This lost essence of *Satori* has led to untold lectures
and a pantheon of written words.

People attempt to capture the nothingness of *Satori*,
making it somethingness.

The moment this happens, Satori *is no more.*

one hundred thirty-four

People tell the world that they have experienced *Satori*—that they have stepped into the realm of abstract No-Mind consciousness.

But by its very nature *Satori* does not last.

Holding it,
describing it,
claiming its obtainment,
causes you to to never experience it again.

Experience once known is sought after again.
Sought after, the unexplained uniqueness of Satori *is lost.*

one hundred thirty-five

For some, touching *Satori* once is all that they need.

From the experience, they claim rank, stature, and having met with the essence of the divine.

Satori *can not be held, no matter how hard you try.*
Satori *can not be mastered, no matter what you do.*
Satori *can not be forced to reoccur, no matter how much you meditate.*
Satori *can only be when* Satori *is.*

one hundred thirty-six

Satori's beauty is its temporariness.

Feel it — let it go,
Know the unknown is knowable and then continue on.

What do you do after Satori?
Live your life.

one hundred thirty-seven

People want to believe that if they touch Cosmic Consciousness they
will never need to do anything ever again. Somehow, some way all of their
needs and desires will be answered.

Your needs and desires are your choice. If you possess simple needs
and desires, they are easily answered. The more you choose to have,
the harder their acquisition.

That is why Zen teaches simplicity.
The simpler, the cheaper.
The cheaper, the easier the obtainment.

With little to obtain, life becomes unadulterated.

This leaves you with no worries.

Let go of believing that Nirvana will answer anything
and you are free.

Free, you can stop seeking and start embracing simplicity.

At the point you meet simplicity, you will pierce the illusion of life.

Seeing is knowing enlightenment.

one hundred thirty-eight

If you can forget about desire and worry for a moment—in that moment you are at peace.

Quiet your mind:
> no desire,
> no worry,
> no care,
> no pain,
> no anguish,
> no remembrance.

Let go and know Nirvana.

one hundred thirty-nine

People play dress-up.

They wear the robes of a monk from an Eastern Culture and hope to appear more enlightened.

Does the clothing you wear make you more enlightened?

one hundred forty

Some people claim that what they wear is a reminder of who and what they strive to become.

If you don't know who you are inside,
what you wear outside has little meaning.

Become enlightenment,
and you will project enlightenment.
Then, the style of your clothing will not matter,
as your inner presence will overshadow your outer apparel.

one hundred forty-one

You can meditate for long hours if you want to meditate.

Meditation places your mind in a cocoon so you do not have
to encounter the unpleasantness of day-to-day reality.

Meditating and renouncing the world has been propagated as a path
to enlightenment. But what does renouncing the world prove?

Renouncing provides nothing but a seemingly holy reason for
running away from the stresses of modern society.

Running away does not equal enlightenment.
Running away equals escapism.
It is easy to be peaceful in a cave.
But how much enlightenment can you find?

See enlightenment in every life action,
and you will find that the essence of true Nirvana
is everywhere and in everything you do,
even those things you do not want to do.

one hundred forty-two

What do you hope to accomplish if you renounce the world?

You won't have to deal with the problems of your job.
You won't have to deal with the emotional roller coaster
      of your relationships.
But, how will you exist?
Who will feed you?
Who will provide you shelter?

*Do you believe that simply because you have renounced the world
that you deserve things to simply be provided for you?*

one hundred forty-three

The worldly person passes through much of their existence striving
for a better life. But, what does it equal? Unfulfilled desires and regrets.

Monks pass through much of their existence striving for enlightenment.
But what does it equal? The realization that they were not pure enough,
holy enough, or possessed enough good Karma to meet Nirvana.

Very different paths,
same outcome.

The key factor—striving.

Let go of striving.
Step into Nirvana.

one hundred forty-four

No matter how seemingly holy your occupation,
Nirvana cannot be captured.

Just because it is written in some scripture that a monk is somehow
holier than the average person, does that mean that it is true?

Just because there is an individual on a pulpit, who you believe to be
an enlightened teacher, does that mean that they are?

Who does more good for the world:
the monk who sits in meditation all day and all night
or the farmer who grows apples to feed you?

Without food, there is no life.
Without life, the contemplation of Nirvana becomes meaningless.

Who wrote the scriptures?
Monks.

Who fed them?
Farmers.

What is the most holy occupation?

one hundred forty-five

Do Buddhist monks care about how they are perceived?

Do Buddhist monks have shaved heads and wear robes?

If they didn't care about how they were perceived, they would not set themselves apart from the rest of the world.

Monkhood is not enlightenment.

Monkhood is simply Monkhood.

one hundred forty-six

To take No Action
sounds like a very Zen statement.
But to take No Action, life ceases to exist.

Life gone,
Nirvana is gone.

Nirvana is a living experience.

Do dead people contemplate Nirvana?

one hundred forty-seven

Knowing more than you
does not mean Absolute Knowledge.

Many people fall under the illusion that a teacher who knows a lot about
a specific subject is enlightened.

Study equals knowledge.
But knowledge does not equal enlightenment.
Enlightenment is the opposite of knowledge.

Knowing this,
let go of knowing this.

one hundred forty-eight

There is no Transmission of Enlightenment.

Nirvana can not be given to you.

It must be Self-Realized.

one hundred forty-nine

A teacher can only take you as far as their ego and the knowledge will allow.

It is you who must finally step into your own Knowing and meet Nirvana.

one hundred fifty

Do to become.
Undo to unbecome.

The first step must be taken
before the second step may be understood.

one hundred fifty-one

Nirvana is being here,
> *without the thought of going there.*

one hundred fifty-two

From Sanskrit, the literal translation of Nirvana is, "Extinction,"
  when who you are ceases to exist.

Next time you think about Nirvana, remember this definition.

  Mentally cease to exist.
  Forget who you think you are.
  Become extinct,
  and you will meet Nirvana.

one hundred fifty-three

Samsara is the endless cycle of rebirth and reincarnation, which only ends when an individual remembers Nirvana.

The *Bodhisatva Vow*—the pledge made by an enlightened individual who promises to return, lifetime after lifetime, to this chaotic earthly existence, until all beings know Nirvana.

Selfless action—the ultimate pathway to Nirvana.

one hundred fifty-four

It is a common practice that many schools of Buddhism lay down all kinds of rules, evaluations, and doctrines for the way a student of Zen should embrace the philosophy.

Do these schools understand the essence of Zen?

Zen is not about formality.
In fact, formality is in direct contrast to Zen.

Zen is about communing with the Supreme Understanding and obtaining Buddhahood. But, this attainment is kept from the student by all of the formalities.

Do the enlightened hold onto formality?
Do the enlightened need ceremonies?
Do the enlightened follow rituals?

No, the enlightened do not.
But those who want to promise step-by-step advancement have a plethora of rules, ceremonies, and rituals.

Many teachers of Zen, do not understand Zen.

Let go of teaching.
Forget formality.
Become the enlightenment of Zen.

one hundred fifty-five

One of the leading distractions to embracing Nirvana is the unnecessary seriousness which many people bring to the Spiritual Path.

"I am on the road to enlightenment, there is no room for frivolity."

Why must spiritual people be sullen?
Why should spiritual people not be able to laugh?

Let go of the false impressions.
Let go of the vision of silent monks meditatively walking through the corridors of some *ashram*, making their way down the path to meet some form of enlightenment where there is no joy.

Nirvana is not serious.
The only people who place unnecessary seriousness upon it are those who have not basked in its pure glory.

Feel its essence, and laugh.

one hundred fifty-six

Once Nirvana is known, all else is forgotten.

Know Nirvana, forget everything else.

one hundred fifty-seven

Nobody can give you Nirvana.

It's a gift you give yourself.